WHEN WAR WAS HECK

PHIL EMMERT

When War Was Heck
Copyright © 2014 Phil Emmert
All Rights Reserved

This book or any portion thereof may not be reproduced without the express written permission of the publisher, except for the use of brief quotations in a book review and certain other noncommercial uses permitted by copyright law.

This is a work of fiction. Names, characters, places, and incidents either are products of the author's imagination or are used fictitiously. Any resemblance to actual events or locales or persons, living or dead, is entirely coincidental.

First edition 2014
Published in the USA by *thewordverve inc.* (**www.thewordverve.com**)

eBook ISBN: 978-1-941251-26-3
Paperback ISBN: 978-1-941251-25-6

Library of Congress Control Number: 2014953580

When War Was Heck
A Book with Verve by thewordverve inc.

Cover and interior design by Robin Krauss
www.bookformatters.com

eBook formatting by Bob Houston
facebook.com/eBookFormatting

DEDICATION

I write this book as a legacy for my children, grandchildren, and all who love freedom and righteousness—in appreciation of the Americans who have gone before us.

FOREWORD

The early 1940s was a time of innocence and naivety. We had seen the ravages of war only in the movies and in the newsreels. But when war came to America in the form of a surprise attack on a place we had never heard of, we grew up fast and became united in our efforts to fight fascism and preserve our freedoms.

This book contains the recollections of World War II on the home front. Through the eyes of a schoolboy, the setting is a small town in central Indiana. Political correctness had not been invented. We talked straight and did not worry about offending people. Japanese were called Japs or Nips. Germans were called Krauts or Huns.

I am over seventy-six years old now, but some of these memories are indelible and I hope to never forget. I have found that men and women my age and above hate war. At the same time, we are the most patriotic and freedom-loving age group in the world. We realize what we could have lost—the freedom we enjoy every day—had it not been for the sacrifices of our finest young people as well as every citizen of America.

My hope is to instill some of the love for freedom in

our young people who have not been taught very much about the most important history in the last one hundred years.

~ Phil Emmert

TABLE OF CONTENTS

1 The Days of Summer 1
2 The Big Move 13
3 The Great Escape 21
4 The Trip out of Town 25
5 The Mystery 31
6 The Perfect Winter 39
7 Battling Bullies 47
8 The Watchdog 51
9 Whistles and Bells 53
Glossary 57

CHAPTER 1

THE DAYS OF SUMMER

Creeping around the side of the weather-beaten house an inch at a time, I hugged the wall and tried to blend in with the late afternoon shadows. If I could just make it to that old cherry tree at the side of the house, I could take aim with my sniper rifle from the branches and pick them off one by one.

Just then, I heard the sound of *rat-a-tat-tat-tat*. Submachine gunfire. The sound was very close to me and was coming from under the bushes that separated two houses. Then a voice blurted out in a high, excited pitch, "I got you! You are dead!" He was right. I never saw or heard him. Dropping my weapon and clutching my chest, I fell to the ground like a sack of potatoes. I gasped one last time and lay there thinking of all the people who would be weeping over my tragic sacrifice. I wondered who would take possession of my "Purple Heart."

After a couple of seconds, I jumped up and shouted, "Okay, I'm alive again."

It was June 10, 1944, in Booneville, Indiana, a small town made up of close-knit neighbors, extended families, and a few old crackpots. Ronnie Neal was my closest friend. He and I were inseparable buddies. We all called him Peanut (I think it was because of the shape of his head). It was he who had just shot me with his homemade wooden submachine gun.

We heard on the radio the night before that there had been a raging battle going on in France since the sixth of June. This battle carried a code name, "D-Day." The report said our guys were moving at a fast pace, and the word was that the war would be over in just a few weeks. Little did we know the war would take another year to end. Peanut, his brother Jimmy, two other boys named Jamie Hand and Dickey Peterson, and I had been reenacting the battle for an unnamed French village.

We all congregated at the lean-to of a back porch attached to the back of our house. I twisted the water faucet and waited for the water to run cold in the old rubber hose. Then I shot a stream of cold water into my mouth and over my face. It was delicious, even though it tasted like rubber.

Next, I squirted a stream at Peanut. He dodged, grabbed the hose, and bent it, shutting off the pressure. Turning off the valve, I ran out in the backyard in time to see Jimmy, Jamie, and Dickey disappearing down the alley toward the Neal house. They were probably going to plot some devious trick on Libby. Libby was Peanut and Jimmy's fifteen-year-old sister. She was tall with long, dark hair and green eyes. I thought she was as pretty as a spotted pup, but her brothers didn't think so.

Peanut announced, "I'm going home and see what's for supper." I acknowledged this information with a snappy salute and marched into the kitchen from the back porch. My sister Mary Anne shot me a look that said *get out of here, you little worm*, as she took a long drink out of a bottle of Coca-Cola. I didn't say anything. She was fourteen and tough for a girl. Besides, I had fought enough battles for one day. I was still a little sore from falling down as if I'd been shot. Walking through the house, I tried to be quiet because my mother was sleeping. She had to work the "graveyard shift" at eleven o'clock. So I needed to be quiet until she got up and stirred around.

Daddy was on the front porch reading the evening paper with a serious look on his face. He had renamed the *Booneville Reporter* to the *Daily Disappointment*. However, I noticed he always grabbed it and read it as soon as the paperboy delivered. The only thing I ever read in that newspaper was the cartoon section, which only had five cartoons. Daddy sat in an old wooden rocker, slowly rocking, reading, and puffing on his pipe. He frowned from time to time, suggesting that he was slightly disturbed about something. I made a mental note not to do anything to disturb Daddy tonight. He was quick to give a whipping when he was like this.

People walked a lot during these last three years since Pearl Harbor. Only the police, sheriff, doctors, and few other important people seemed to drive much these days. Due to rationing, it just wasn't worth the trouble to drive. Daddy sold our Model A Ford with the neat rumble seat when we moved to town two years before. From time to time, a neighbor or an acquaintance walked by while Daddy was reading the paper. They would stop to chat and exchange news about the war or the prospects for the weather.

I sat on the front step with the warm sun on my face. It would be another hour before it would be below the trees across the street. Old Buck, our faithful black and white border collie, nuzzled his nose under my arm and licked me on the side of the face. He really knew how to pick up the spirits of a wounded soldier. This was the life: a front porch, the sun on your face, and a good dog at your side.

A car pulled up at the house next door. It was Mr. Cunningham, the high school principal, bringing Shirley home. Shirley was the neighbor's unmarried daughter. Shirley was also Mr. Cunningham's secretary at the school. They always sat and talked for a long time before she went in the house. I guess they were not able to talk at school. I also decided Mr. Cunningham must have been hard of hearing, because they always sat real close together in the car. Since school had been out almost two weeks, they must have had a lot of extra work to do. I wondered if Mr. Cunningham's wife was holding supper for him.

I finally got tired of old Buck putting his tongue in my ear, so I decided to skate around the block and see what was going on. I retrieved my roller skates from the closet under the stairway and clamped them onto my old shoes. I guessed I must have put about a hundred miles on those skates since school let out. I started north up Oak Street so I could get a better look at Mr. Cunningham and Shirley in his blue 1940 Chevy. They stopped talking and moved apart as I skated even with the car. I waved at them and skated on. Shirley waved weakly and started to open the car door.

Crossing the alley, I stopped to talk with Mrs. Dillon and her daughter Imogene. I hoped Imogene noticed my skating ability. She was cute as a button, and her dad owned the grocery store just down the block and around the corner. Mrs. Wilson, who was an elderly widow, waved at me from across the street. She, like Daddy, was sitting on her porch reading the paper. I liked Mrs. Wilson. In the winter, she would give me a dime (sometimes a quarter) to take her coal ashes out on Saturdays.

Around the block once and I was so hot I took off my skates and went to the "icebox" in the kitchen to check out the ice situation. There wasn't much left, and the iceman would not come until tomorrow. I chipped some ice off with an ice pick and let the pieces melt in my mouth. Man, that was refreshing. Mary Anne had guzzled the last Coke, so I would have to wait until I sold some soft drink bottles to buy one. I could have begged a nickel off Daddy but thought better of it—due to his unpredictable mood this evening.

Daddy and Momma both worked at Winkler's. Winkler's was a factory that made coal stokers before the war. There were two Winkler brothers. They came up with the idea for an "automatic stoker" so you wouldn't have to keep shoveling coal into your furnace. Only rich people had furnaces. Really rich people now had stokers. We heated our house with a "Warm Morning" cast iron coal stove. Well, anyway, these Winkler brothers were about as German as you could get, but everyone in town accepted them because they were helping with the war effort. Besides that, they had been naturalized, whatever in the world that meant. I thought our neighbor might have had that done to his cat once. The Winkler factory now made 75 mm "mortar shells." The factory ran three shifts to turn out shells. Everyone in town that was "4-F," or not engaged in some other war effort, seemed to work at Winkler's factory.

Directly, Daddy came in from the porch and made us some supper of bologna sandwiches and milk. He also scrounged up some vanilla cookies from somewhere.

We sat at the table eating our bologna sandwiches and drinking our milk. We didn't say anything. We were each lost in our own thoughts about what it would be like when the war was over. I sneaked three cookies in my pocket for later. Two for me and one for Buck.

Momma got up just before I went to bed. She ate and made a sandwich to take to work. Just as she was asking me about my day, the town fire siren went off and we turned out all the lights. It was only a "blackout" drill. We didn't have heavy black drapes, so we had to turn out our lights completely. The town turned off the lights along the street and in the businesses at nine o'clock. It was kind of nice to sit on the front porch in the dark and listen to the night sounds. There were just a few lightning bugs. In a couple of weeks, there would be thousands of them. The neighborhood kids would have a contest to see who could catch the most. You could almost light a room with a jar of lightning bugs.

The next morning I awoke early, before Momma got home from work. I went to the backyard and looked for the baseball I had left there yesterday. Drying off the dew, I tossed it on the roof and caught it a few times. Working up an appetite, I went in the kitchen and ate some cornflakes without sugar. We were out of sugar and couldn't get any more until the new ration stamps were issued on the fifteenth of the month. Man, I wished we had some sugar.

Just then I heard a knock on the screen door as Peanut said, "Hey, buddy, what do you want to do this morning?" It was a question that really didn't require an answer. I had a most undesirable job as soon as the dew got off the grass. Once a week, I had to mow the yard. Every week, I put it off as long as possible. When I rolled my eyes and nodded at the backyard, Peanut said, "Well, I'll see you later, buddy." All that morning, I would mow a while, and then I would get a drink of water from the rubber hose on the back porch. A Briggs & Stratton engine didn't power this lawnmower. There was no such animal in 1944. No-sir-ee-bob! A sixty-pound bundle of energy powered this old reel-type push mower. One could hear the huffing, puffing, grunting, and the soft whirr of the blades clipping the thick carpet of grass.

About eleven o'clock, a wonderful sight materialized. Behold, the iceman cometh. The card in the kitchen window indicated my mother wanted twenty-five pounds of ice delivered. I ran to the ice truck in the alley. It was a coal black 1935 Ford pickup with a wooden bed. The truck was loaded with huge blocks of ice, covered with thick canvas.

The iceman must have been one of the strongest men I ever beheld. Strangely enough, his name was Mr. Armstrong. He was dressed in denim overalls and high-top leather shoes. He wore a leather apron that strapped to each leg like the chaps of a gunfighter in the old west. On each hand, he wore a leather glove. He carried an ice pick in a sheaf at his hip. He would deftly divide the one-hundred-pound blocks of ice into twenty-five- or fifty-pound chunks and then carry the desired chunk in the house, where he loaded it into the icebox. He could carry a fifty-pound block as if it were a loaf of bread. I stood at the tailgate of the truck as he slivered off the ice. I let the chips melt in my mouth to quench my thirst. It was a ritual that took place three times a week in the summer. This scene was repeated at every house that had an icebox and where kids were present. He was a real-life hero for every kid in town. It kind of made me feel sorry for people who had a refrigerator.

Sometimes in the summer we would walk or skate to the park and swim in the public pool. It provided an afternoon of recreation for the paltry sum of fifteen cents. So that afternoon I felt I had earned a swim. Peanut and I begged fifty cents from his mom and went to the pool. We spent the afternoon swandiving and cannonballing any girl who came into range of the high dive. On the way home, we had enough money left to visit the concession stand. We split a box of popcorn and each drank an ice-cold bottle of Coca-Cola.

That evening Daddy turned on the big RCA Victor radio in the front room and listened to Gabriel Heatter give an update on the war. Then we tuned to *Fibber McGee and Molly*. Later we caught the *Amos and Andy* program. Mary Anne insisted that she listen to some pop songs for the rest of the evening.

One night I walked in and caught Mary Anne dancing with her imaginary boyfriend. She said she would teach me to dance if I would dance with her. I protested but finally gave in and let her teach me to jitterbug. One could jitterbug without touching your partner. I never did let her teach me to foxtrot or to waltz since you had to put your arm around your partner. Yuk! I just couldn't make myself do that.

Usually one night a week, my sister and I would go to the Avon Theater uptown. This theater was plush. It had padded seats, thick carpets, and a marquee with so many lights it could light up that whole end of town. This theater showed only the best pictures, featuring stars such as Clark Gable, Tyrone Power, Jimmy Stewart, Gary Cooper, and my favorite, Lassie. The show was expensive. It cost fifty cents for children and seventy-five cents for adults.

Saturday afternoons were always an "occasion," summer or winter. Peanut and I would go the Saturday matinee at the Lido Theater. For thirty-five cents, we could go to the picture show, buy a box of popcorn, and a cup of ice-cold Coca-Cola. We sat with wide-eyed wonder as

Tom Mix, William Cassidy, Gene Autry, Roy Rogers, and Whip Wilson beat up all the bad guys. You could tell the good guys from the bad guys because the bad guys always wore dark hats.

Sometimes it was scary just getting to the Lido. It was located on the seedy side of town. We had to pass a row of beer joints (saloons) to get to the theater. They played loud music on the jukebox and talked and laughed real loud. Cigar and cigarette smoke bellowed out the swinging doors like smoke from a volcano. We would walk fast and try not to look in as we passed the door, just like our parents told us to do. However, on the way back home, we pretended as if we were one of our western heroes walking down the street of a wild western town. Peanut and I would wink at each other, smile, and say, "We could tame this town if the townspeople would only hire us."

It was in this setting where I learned that life is in constant change. Good or bad, life is like the weather. It will change if we wait a while. I suppose all children would like to live forever in their childhood state. But God never intended for us to stagnate in childhood.

In just a little over a year, the war would be over. My uncles and cousin would be home from serving their country. They would come back wiser, more mature, and never quite as carefree and playful as before. My daddy would change jobs, and my mother would be home for a while. Peanut would move away. Old Buck would die when he became blind and deaf and wandered into the path of a car. So I would not hear Peanut say, "What do you want to do today, buddy?" Nor would I feel Buck's soft muzzle against my cheek when I needed comfort.

CHAPTER 2

THE BIG MOVE

Summer 1941

Clop, clop, clop. The sound of the hooves on the driveway could be heard from down in the dry sand pit where Mary Anne and I were playing. We scurried up the steep slope and caught sight of Daddy bringing the team to the water trough. The team consisted of two huge, perfectly matched Belgian draft horses. Daddy managed the farm where we lived for Mr. Miller, who was an attorney out of Indianapolis. We ran full tilt to where Daddy was pumping water for Millie and Tilley. He stopped pumping and lifted me as if I were a feather and set me on the back of Tilley. She stopped slurping for an instant but never lifted her head. Daddy then lifted Mary Anne up onto Millie's back. Tilley was hot and sweaty from cultivating all day in the corn. She had that sweet wonderful smell that I loved when I put my nose against her hide. Mary held the hames on Millie's harness. I stretched out on the wide, slightly swayed back of old Tilley.

It was six o'clock on that Friday evening in July 1941 when Mr. Miller came roaring up in his dark green 1940 Packard. As the dust settled, he stepped out of the car, slowly scanning the barnyard and then gazed toward the cornfields. He waved and smiled at us. He sometimes teased me, because when he asked my name. I would reply, "Nothing." He'd say, "How are you, Nothing?"

He reached up, tickling Mary Anne on the ribs. To Daddy he said "The farm really looks good, Robert." Reaching into his inside suit pocket, he handed Daddy the familiar brown envelope, which he gave Daddy every Friday. "You'll find a little extra in your pay today for doing such a good job." Daddy took pride in his work. He took care of the farm as if it were his own.

Then Mr. Miller frowned and said, "Robert, you shouldn't let the kids ride on the workhorses. They might throw them or run off with them."

Daddy smiled. "Mr. Miller, them horses have been worked so hard today they don't have the energy to buck or to run." The next day about nine in the morning, Fletcher, Mr. Miller's son, came riding up on Queen, his fancy riding horse. He was leading a beautiful, slick-coated bay pony, complete with an English riding saddle.

He said, "Father sent this pony to you for the kids to ride, so they won't have to ride those workhorses." He added, "His name is Prince."

We came to find out that Prince had been a jumping

champion. Momma found out the hard way, when she went to bring the milk cow up to the barn one night. Momma had been taking Mary Anne and me for a ride on Prince. Since it was getting close to milking time, Momma took Prince to the woods pasture to bring in our one milk cow. Bessie was standing beside an old, downed tree, and it sure must have looked like a jump to Prince. He had been taught if he was headed toward a jump, he was supposed to jump it. Momma kept pulling his head around to keep him from jumping. Well, old Prince just swung around and headed toward the old tree again and again. Finally, Daddy saw what was going on and came to Momma's rescue.

That was the summer I turned seven. Mary Anne and I spent long hours in the dry sand pit behind our house. We built castles, fashioned sand cakes, and sometimes I just moved sand from one place to another with my toy truck. Mary Anne pretended she was a movie star, sunning herself on a beach.

The only time we ever rode Prince was if we rode with Momma or Daddy. We found out Prince was not very fond of kids. When Momma and Daddy weren't looking, Prince would turn his head around and nip us on the leg.

One day Aunt Clara was riding Prince, when he decided he wanted to go to the barn. He got the bit in his teeth and took off at a fast trot. He seemed to break into a full gallop when he reached the open barn door. Aunt Clara grabbed an overhead beam and swung off just as he ran between a corn picker and a hay manger. Well, sir, he ripped the stirrups right off that fancy English saddle. If Aunt Clara had not caught hold of that beam, she could have had her legs broken.

After that, Daddy put Prince out to pasture, and Mary Anne and I rode the workhorses from the water trough to the barn every evening. Daddy told Mr. Miller, "That old Prince was full of the devil."

Daddy had always farmed with horses or mules. Mr. Miller wanted his farm to be more modern, so one fall day, he had a big, red F-20 Farmall tractor delivered to the farm. Daddy looked at it as if it smelled bad or something. He only used it when he knew Mr. Miller was coming to the farm. He made several excuses for not using that tractor. He said it packed the soil too much, and it didn't obey his commands very well. He said, "It wouldn't gee, haw, or giddyup, and it sure wouldn't whoa." One day we heard Daddy hollering, "Whoa! Whoa! Dang it, whoa!" Well, he finally got that big red machine stopped about two inches from a closed gate. Daddy sighed, took off his hat, and wiped his brow with his red bandana.

I guess Daddy's salvation concerning the farm came just about three months later, in early December 1941. It was a horrible day for America, but it caused Daddy to rethink his vocation.

★

December 7, 1941

President Roosevelt called it a Day of Infamy. As I recall, it started out as a wonderful day. We went to Mom and Pop's for Sunday dinner. Mom and Pop were Momma's parents. They had raised four girls and a boy—the old-fashioned way. They did not spare the rod. They were stern disciplinarians, but we loved going there. Pop farmed about fifteen miles from where we lived. We rode over there on that clear crisp Sunday in our Model A Ford. Mary Anne and I played games and took turns swinging on the rope swing hanging from one of the large trees in the yard.

Mom always prepared a huge meal when company came. On Sundays, she would make enough so that she did not have to cook again in the evening. We all ate until our stomachs hurt. Then we ate a little more.

After spreading a white tablecloth over the leftover portions of food, we went to the living room where the adults made plans for Christmas. Mary Anne and I fussed with each other about what Santa was going to bring us. Finally, Daddy said, "If you kids don't be quiet, I'll give you something you don't want," as he reached to unfasten his belt buckle. Well, sir, you never saw two kids shut up any quicker. Daddy never spoke to us twice about the same offense. The second time, he let his belt do the talking. I understood that language all too well.

Sometime between one and two in the afternoon, the telephone began to ring one long continuous ring. This was the way people on the party line knew there was some kind of emergency. It was the way the whole neighborhood was alerted to a house fire or someone needing help. When it rang like this, everyone on the party line would get on and listen.

Mom picked up the receiver, and an excited voice on the other end said, "Turn on your radio, the Japanese have attacked Pearl Harbor." We turned on Pop's old Philco radio and waited for it to warm up. We heard a serious-sounding announcer say that a group of Japanese planes had damaged several American Navy ships at Pearl Harbor.

At seven years of age, I had no idea of the seriousness of such an attack. I only knew that the adults in the room were very upset. Pop said something like, "This means war." The rest of the afternoon and evening, we sat listening to the announcer give a few more details. The telephone would ring from time to time as relatives or friends called to see if we had heard about the attack.

That night, I went to sleep on the ride back home with my head on the shoulder of my mother. I felt secure between the muscular body of my dad and the warmth of my mother. No enemy could touch me there.

Moving On

Before the spring plowing began, our family loaded down the Model A and my uncle's old truck with everything we owned.

As we drove down the lane and out the gate, I took one last look at the only place I could ever remember living. Millie, Tilley, and Prince stood with their heads over the fence staring at what must have looked like a bunch of modern settlers moving west. It was the last time I saw these beautiful animals.

Years later as a young man, I sometimes drove out to the "Miller Place" just to recapture some old memories. But of course, you can never go home again. Besides that, I had new memories to make.

We unloaded all our worldly possessions at 415 North Oak Street—an ancient-looking, two-story house that needed a coat of paint. Sad to say, that old house never got a new coat of paint in the ten years we lived there. Daddy's old maid Aunt Lula owned the house. She rented it to us for practically nothing. As we unloaded and set up furniture, I noticed a boy, who looked to be about my age, supervising our labor. He was a wiry little fellow wearing a GI haircut on his oddly shaped head. In fact, his head reminded me of a peanut. He had a dark tan for so early in the spring. He had bright blue eyes and freckles scattered across his nose. He looked a lot like the pictures I had seen of a leprechaun. I paused, waved, and said, "Hey."

He said, "Hi, buddy, my name's Ronnie, but you can call me Peanut." I couldn't keep from snickering aloud. Somehow, I just knew his nickname had to be Peanut. From that day until Ronnie moved away five years later, he never called me anything but Buddy, and I always called him Peanut.

CHAPTER 3

THE GREAT ESCAPE

Our old, two-story house on North Oak Street looked like it belonged on the other end of town, where all of the houses needed paint and repair. The dilapidated house sat between a lovely, gray stucco bungalow, with an immaculate yard and a well-kept brick house. However, what our house lacked in beauty it made up in character.

The upstairs was scary to me when we first moved in. My sister slept in the front bedroom, and I slept in the back bedroom. Those two rooms were separated by a narrow hallway. The ceilings sloped at about a forty-five-degree angle. On each side of the room under the slope of the roof was an attic that could be entered if you were small like me. I never entered it, however, unless an adult was nearby. It was dark and had a musty smell to it.

In the winter, if my mother wanted to dry clothes quickly for use the next day, she hung them on a clothesline stretched across my room from one corner to another. This divided my room, with the clothes being the dividing wall. Often Momma would hang Daddy's long underwear or his overalls on that line. Late at night, I would come awake and peek out from under the cover to see a long, white object suspended in air. It looked like a ghost that was ready to attack me in my bed. I would put my head under my cover and try to breathe ever so softly, not moving a muscle. I could hear my heart beating and was sure it would give me away as it beat loudly and rapidly. Sometimes I would lie awake for what seemed like hours before falling back to sleep. I might hear a car going down the street, such as a police car on patrol. When I heard a car, I would peek from under the cover as the headlights traversed the room and finally exposed the ghost. It was always the clothes hanging on the line.

Momma finally came to my rescue when she found out I was terrified by these imaginary monsters in my room. She attached a string to the chain on the bare light bulb hanging in the center of the room. She tied the other end of the string to the head rail on my cot. When I awoke and was frightened in the night, I quickly pulled the string and immediately the monsters turned back into Daddy's clothes. I would fall asleep again with the light on.

There was a cherry tree at one corner of the house (more about it later) and a very skinny elm tree at another corner. This elm tree sat very close to the kitchen and the side porch. From my upstairs bedroom, I could crawl out the window and make my way down the slope of the roof to that skinny tree. I could then slide down the tree and escape from the house. The difficult part was getting back up the tree. I was probably twelve years old before I was strong enough to shinny up that tree to sneak back into the house.

Summer nights in Indiana were hot and stifling. The only air conditioning in those days were small fans and open windows. After going to bed, it would be so hot in my upstairs room that I would lie on the flat part of the roof just outside my window. It was during one of these dreadfully hot nights that I discovered this easy exit from the house. It became so easy that even in the mornings, I would dress and slide down the tree like a fireman down a fire pole. This was my escape from the house. Nevertheless, I had another escape that was even more exciting for me. It was my escape from the real world.

This adventure involved the other tree. It was a cherry tree, but I have never seen one like it since. The fruit came on in midsummer. Instead of being red and tart like "normal" cherries, the fruit was yellow and sweet as sugar when ripe. Summer or winter, however, that tree was my escape from the real world. When the world mistreated me, I would climb up into that cherry tree and sit on one particular limb. The bark on that limb became smooth from the seat of my pants. There I would sit and pretend I was somewhere else and someone else.

In my new world, I was always rich with nice clothes

and lived in a mansion. All the girls thought I was handsome, and I would end up rescuing them from some danger.

When I was particularly distressed, I talked to some being, some presence I never could identify. He always listened to me and brought me comfort on the limb of that old cherry tree. Years later, I found that friend. His name was Jesus. Somehow, God must have planted that tree just for me. When I climbed down out of that tree, I always felt refreshed.

There are times I still yearn for that cherry tree with its yellow cherries. The tree is long gone, but the memory lingers.

CHAPTER 4

THE TRIP OUT OF TOWN

Early one spring morning in 1943, the house was alive with anticipation. Momma and Daddy both had three days off from the factory. Even old Buck knew something was up. Everyone was up and out of bed at the same time. Buck sat on the front porch looking in the screen door, cocking his head to one side as if he was asking a question. Momma was in the kitchen making each of us a peanut butter and jelly sandwich. She wrapped each sandwich in waxed paper and placed them in a brown paper grocery bag. Mary Anne was primping, brushing her hair, and looking at herself in the mirror. I thought, *She is going to break that mirror someday with her ugly self.* Daddy was pacing back and forth, checking his pocket watch every five minutes. Every time he looked at his watch, he would call out the time.

Finally, at ten minutes after seven, we walked out the door and onto the sidewalk, while Daddy shut the wooden door. We never locked the house. I'm not sure we even had a door key. Earlier I had given Buck fresh water and a handful of last night's supper scraps. He would make his neighborhood rounds to get some more to eat later. Buck belonged to us, but the neighbors had all adopted him. All of them fed him their best table scraps. Buck plopped down on the porch, crossed his front paws, and laid his head on them. He managed to roll his big, brown eyes upward and look so sad. We'd just never all left at one time before.

The four of us began our six-block walk south down Oak Street toward the train station. I pretended I was riding a horse. I galloped ahead of everybody. Then I would rein in and come back at a trot. Momma and Daddy were preoccupied in conversation. Mary Anne rolled her eyes and told Momma to make me stop acting so dumb. I pulled out my imaginary Colt .45 and aimed it at her. Momma caught sight of this imaginary threat. She swatted my backside with her purse and gave me that look mommas can give. I deftly twirled and holstered my trusty revolver.

As we arrived at the Big Four Railway Station, a huge crowd was milling about. I never saw so many servicemen in my life. Army, Marine, and Navy uniforms were everywhere. The train had arrived a few minutes earlier. The servicemen had gotten off to stretch their legs and visit the restroom. Daddy bought four tickets and the stationmaster said, "Remember, you may have to stand up. Our soldiers get to ride first class."

Just then, the conductor called out, "All aboard," in an accent that sounded foreign. He sure wasn't a Hoosier. We all moved forward in a shuffling motion until we came to the train steps. A young Marine reached down, picked me up, and stood me on the train platform. I looked around as a sailor did the same with Mary Anne. She was giggling while I thought, *Man, he must be really strong to pick up that load.* An older sergeant with service stripes and a bunch of campaign ribbons on his chest set his duffel bag in the aisle. He motioned me to sit on it. Some other men got up and insisted that Momma and Mary Anne sit down.

The train started with a lurch as all coal-fired steam engines started. Soon, the Indiana farmland was rushing past the window with a clickety-clack of the wheels on the rails. This was the first and only time I ever rode a train—a thrill beyond description,

We were on our way to Indianapolis to visit my Aunt Ruth. Her husband, Uncle Clarence, was somewhere overseas, if he was still alive. Indianapolis was only thirty miles away, but we would stop two more times before we arrived. Every serviceman on the train tried to give Mary Anne and me all kinds of goodies. By the time we got to Indianapolis, we had candy bars, chewing gum, and apples in our pockets. Forget about the peanut butter and jelly sandwiches! Some of the servicemen just wanted to pat us on the head and tell us how precious we were. I noticed some of the older soldiers had tears in their eyes. It was only after I had children of my own that I would understand the tears.

Upon our arrival in Indianapolis, Aunt Ruth picked us up in her 1939 Ford. We stayed with her that day and the next. Momma and Aunt Ruth did some shopping in downtown Indianapolis. The next day, Aunt Ruth drove us back home. She said she had been saving her gas-ration stamps for such an occasion. Daddy bought the gas. You see, one had to have the gas-ration stamps, but you also had to have the money to pay for the gas. Needless to say, there was a black market for everything that was rationed. If you knew who to talk to, and if you had enough money, you could buy all those things for an elevated price. It was sad, but some people got rich off the misery of war.

Our trip in Aunt Ruth's car was a wiz bang. Old US 52 was a concrete road. Every thirty feet or so, the road had an asphalt expansion seam. When you hit that seam, it went bump. At certain speeds, it felt like a flat tire. Well, sir, we were moving right along at the speed limit of thirty-five miles per hour. We were talking and looking at the scenery. That old Ford was perking right along, bumpity-bump, bumpity-bump. Aunt Ruth said, "I think I have a flat tire." We all howled because she always said that when she drove old US 52. We had all made wagers about how long it would take her to say that. She pulled off, and she checked one side while Daddy checked the other side. Nope, all the tires were fine. We drove on another five miles or so, and Aunt Ruth said, "I really do think I have a flat tire." We checked them again. We did this four times in thirty miles.

CHAPTER 5

THE MYSTERY

One night Daddy came home late after working two shifts. He was dead tired, but he was also hungry. He went to the icebox and got out the milk and some minced ham for a sandwich. He made a couple of sandwiches and drank a glass of milk. He was so tired he just put the meat and milk in the icebox and left the bread on the table. He went right to bed and was out like a light in short order.

Next morning, Mary Anne went down to fix some toast and drink a glass of milk. I heard her holler, "William Henry!" I was already outside on the front step, trying to get Buck to sit up. He had "lie down" and "play dead" down pat. Matter of fact, that's about all he could do. Well, when Mary Anne bellowed like a sick calf, I figured she had found her lipstick that I had used to write "Kilroy was here" on our clubhouse. I was wrong. She didn't find that out until a day or so later. I went into the kitchen with my most innocent expression on my face. Mary Anne shouted, "What did you do with the milk and bread?"

I said, "Who, me?"

She said, "Yeah, you little twit!"

Well, I did not know what a twit was, but I was pretty sure I wasn't one. So I simply said, "Sis, I didn't have the milk and bread. Not only that, you better be quiet before Daddy wakes up and beats both of us."

She said, "Well, we had a whole loaf of bread and a full quart of milk last evening. I know Daddy didn't eat and drink all of that last night."

I looked in the icebox. Sure enough, the milk, bottle, and all were gone. Then I noticed the minced ham was gone too. I went to the store yesterday and bought all that stuff, and some cookies too. Let's see, a quart of milk (bottle and all), a whole loaf of bread, and a pound of minced ham were all gone. I opened the cabinet, and man, would you believe it, the cookies were all gone too. Beating or not, we needed to tell Daddy.

"You go."

"No, you tell him."

Well, this went on for about five minutes. Finally, we heard, "What in the Sam Hill is going on in there?" I didn't want Daddy to have to ask again, because I have a real low threshold for pain. So I ran in and gave Daddy a rundown on what we found this morning (or what we didn't find.) I also reassured him he could smell my breath. There was no ham, milk, or cookies on it. He said he was too tired to do anything about it right now. He continued, "Go get some more at Dillon's Store and tell Ed to put it on our bill."

I could hardly wait to tell Peanut about this crime—right in our own house. After picking up the items at the store, I went down to Peanut's house. Jimmy, Dickie, and Jamie were trying to get up a basketball game in the back alley. The Neals had a really nice goal fastened securely to the garage in the back alley. It even had a net on it. We played basketball almost every day.

As soon as I could get Peanut off by himself, I told him about our mystery. I playfully asked to smell his breath, then I said, "Man, don't you ever brush your teeth?" We went back to our house and did some detective work. There was very little grass in our side yard up close to the house. It had drizzled the night before. We examined the ground beneath the kitchen window. Someone had stood facing the window recently. Whoever it was sure was not a kid. They had big feet. I would judge about a size eleven. The pattern of the print was strange too. There was an odd marking on both shoes. It looked a lot like a German swastika. One of the little feet of the crooked cross was missing, but other than that, it sure looked like one.

If I had not been wearing a GI haircut, my hair would have stood right straight on end anyway. I looked at Peanut. He was pale as a ghost, even though he had a summer tan. We were both thinking of a recent Pathe newsreel we had seen at the Avon Theater. US citizens were warned to be on the lookout for escaped German POWs. We heard that there were several hundred housed at Camp Atterbury. This camp was only about sixty miles south of Boonville as the crow flies. We put the scenario together in our little ten-year-old minds. A German POW had escaped. He could have ridden the rails to Boonville and come into the residential area looking for food. If he was desperate, it was hard telling what he would do. We had heard some really scary stories about those Germans. I said to Peanut, "Let's act like we are playing, but let's look in all the garages, coal sheds, and basements around the neighborhood. No one locks their garages or coal sheds, and I can get into any basement in the neighborhood."

Peanut and I acted as if we were playing Army. We had our wooden guns as we began our search. I figured we might as well start in my own backyard. I crouched low and pretended to toss a grenade into the coal shed. Peanut ran to the opening where the coal was loaded into the shed. I ran to the other end and threw open the door. Man, I sure hoped he wasn't in here.

All I had was this wooden handmade M-1. It didn't even begin to look real. Peanut's wooden submachine gun looked even more ridiculous. Our grenades were the most dangerous weapon in our arsenal. Green apples. Yes, we carried green apples for grenades. They could hurt you two ways—one, if they hit you in the right spot and, even worse, if you ate too many of them. Well, our "Kraut" friend wasn't in our coal shed. We continued our methodical search of every coal shed, garage, and basement in the 300 and 400 blocks of Oak Street. We were clean. We were clean in more ways than one. Peanut and I had to clean Widow Wilson's basement to search it. She was a pretty sharp lady.

Peanut and I walked uptown to look at comic books at the drugstore. We didn't have any money, but we could look until Doc, the druggist, came out and said, "Okay, boys, buy some or move on." On our way, whom should we meet but Big John Small? His name was Officer Small, but all the adults called him Big John because he sure was not small. Peanut and I called him "Sir."

Big John was walking his beat, which was around the town square. We waved at him, and he stopped to talk with us as he always did. I began to tell him about our mystery. I think he thought I was crazy. He just kind of had a little smile on his lips. When I finished telling him the whole thing, he said, "Well, boys, let's walk over to the station house and pick up a car." We went to the police station, and he told the dispatcher he was going to take one of the cars for a little bit. He said, "Come on, boys, let's go for a ride."

I wasn't supposed to get in a car with someone who wasn't family, but I guessed Officer Small was okay. Where did we go? We went right square to my house. We got out, and he said, "Show me the footprints." He studied them a while and said "Boys, you might have something here."

About that time, Daddy came out wiping the sleep from his eyes. He said, "Well, Big John, do we have a crime on our hands or what?"

Officer Small said, "If you're missing some food, I guess we do."

Daddy confirmed what was missing.

That night the Boonville Police and the sheriff's department cruised up and down the streets and alleys. In a few days, we began to feel safe again. Then about a month later, as we were playing basketball at the Neal house, a strange man came down the alley. He was dressed in ragged clothes that were too big for him. He looked like an old man, but as he got closer, we observed that he wasn't as old as he appeared from a distance. He was looking in all the garbage cans in the alley. When he thought we were not looking, he would peek in a garage window. We watched him guardedly as he passed where we were playing. We avoided eye contact but noted all we could about him. I noticed he had stepped out of the alley in a place or two where there was some fresh sand. After he was almost to my house, I walked over to the fresh sand and checked out the footprint. I frantically motioned

Peanut to come look. There in the sand was the very same print that we saw at our kitchen window. It was the same size and with the same strange, crooked-cross markings. This was our man.

The Neals had a telephone. Peanut had his mother call the police station. She reported there was a strange man walking the alley in the 400 block between Oak and Main streets. It couldn't have been more than two minutes when a black and white 1940 Plymouth police car came slowly down our alley. We pointed in the direction of the man. We could barely see him still walking slowly, checking trash bins and garbage cans.

We watched as the police car stopped and the officer got out. We fully expected to see a struggle, but it didn't happen. The man got into the car under his own power. The car slowly turned around and came back down the alley, stopping in front of us. Officer Small asked, "Is this the man?" We nodded and tried not to look too closely at him. We were really scared. We sure hoped he wouldn't suddenly pull out a German luger and start shooting. But the man looked as scared as we did. Officer Small drove off toward the jail.

The next day it was all over town that a strange man was in jail for vagrancy. I didn't know what that meant, but I remember thinking it must be a horrible crime. Sometime later, we learned that the man was not a German POW. He was a US citizen from out west somewhere. He was drafted into the Army and then went AWOL because he didn't want to fight. Peanut and I just couldn't understand someone who wouldn't fight the Krauts or the Japs. He deserved to eat out of garbage cans.

Daddy didn't press charges against him. He said, "That young man has enough problems without me adding to them." I reckoned Daddy was right. Anyway, he wouldn't be stealing anything out of our icebox again. We never did find out about the strange marks on the bottom of his shoes. That's still an unsolved mystery.

CHAPTER 6

THE PERFECT WINTER

Momma and Daddy were not very fond of winter. Just heating a house and keeping pipes from freezing in Indiana became a chore. However, as a child, winter could be a very special season. Soon after Halloween, I awoke each morning, anticipating the first snowfall.

The day before Thanksgiving 1944, my eyes came open as I heard Daddy stoking the Warm Morning stove in the living room. It seemed extra cold in my room upstairs. Thankfully, the chimney ran up through the floor in my room. Therefore, my room warmed up more quickly than Mary Anne's room, and it was the last to cool down at night.

I peeked out from under the thick quilt as I heard the rush of the flames shooting up the chimney. Daddy always threw a tin can full of coal oil in the stove to get it going quickly in the morning. I turned my head toward the window, blinked once, threw the cover back, and vaulted from bed in one swift motion. SNOW! Precious, delicious, wonderful snow! It lay on the flat part of the roof that projected out from my window. There must have been four inches on this roof already, and it was still snowing.

I gathered my pants, shirt, and socks from the foot of my bed. Scrambling down the stairs and jumping the last three steps, I quickly dressed between the wall and the Warm Morning stove. It was always nice and toasty dressing there on a cold morning. I had learned to take care, however. I still had a big ugly scar on my tender backside, where I fell against the stove two years before.

Slipping on my shoes, which I had left near the stove the night before, I ran to the front porch. Reaching down on the bottom step, I scooped up a double handful of the soft, wet snow, forming it into a cold, hard projectile. I looked around for a target. The only one I saw was the Chinese elm tree in front of the house on the curbside of the sidewalk. It was a young tree, only about a foot around. I squinted, wound up, and let it fly. Bull's eye! It was going to be a great winter.

I was so excited that morning I couldn't eat. I had to be reminded to take out the ashes and bring in a bucket of coal from the coal shed. Momma said, "Billy Boy, put on your mittens."

"But Mom, you can't make a decent snowball with mittens."

Momma gave me that look that said, *William Henry,*

don't you dare say another word. I swallowed my protest and put on my mittens.

Meeting Peanut at his house on the way to Harney Elementary School, I noticed he was as excited as I was. We threw snowballs at each other and at any girl we spied on the way to school. We ran and slid on the new snow and tried to pack it down. If we could pack it down, it would be real slick by the time school was out that afternoon.

We arrived at Harney, which was a large, brick, foreboding structure. It had two floors dedicated to classrooms and the principal's office. It had a large basement, which housed the restrooms and the furnace with, of course, a Winkler Stoker. The rumor was that the attic-like third floor stored supplies. Personally, I suspected the ghosts of teachers who had died long ago resided there. I also suspected it was these ghosts who misplaced my homework and broke the lead in my pencil at inopportune times.

The building sat in the corner of a large corner lot. The rest of the lot was playground. We had no swings, slides, or teeter totters. There was a wire backstop where we played kickball. Covering the grassless playground were small pebbles, called pea gravel. At every recess, someone had to have little pebbles picked out of the palms of their hands or out of a skinned knee. When this happened to Peanut or me, we pretended it was shrapnel from a hand grenade.

Each morning, Miss O'Rear, the principal, always met the children at one of the main entrances. One entrance was on the east side, which was my entrance. On the west side, there was another entrance. Miss O'Rear would be at one door or the other, with a stern look that seemed to say: *I don't like kids very much, and if you step out of line, I'll eat you for breakfast.*

Speaking of eating, there was no lunchroom and no free lunch. A kid either went home to eat lunch or he brought a sandwich and ate it at his desk. We did have milk, which cost a nickel for a half-pint glass bottle of whole milk. This milk always had thick cream on the top.

All that winter of 1944-45, it was extremely cold, with a lot of ice and snow. The boots I wore the winter before no longer fit. Rubber boots were hard to come by. Our soldiers needed the rubber more than we did. All the sliding on the ice and snow had worn a hole in the bottom of my leather-soled shoes. I would probably get a new pair at Christmas. In the meantime, Momma cut out cardboard and lined my shoes. She had to do this every day or so, because in the ice, snow, and slush, the cardboard got soaked. But when you're ten years old, your feet do not seem to get cold as you play, romp, and slide in the snow.

Peanut and I built a fabulous snow fort in December, which lasted until almost April. We built it on the north side of our house, and the sun never hit it. Our fort just got icier and harder. We kept building it up with each new snowfall. On the Saturday morning after we built our fort, we spent about an hour making and stockpiling ammunition. Our fort faced the sidewalk, side yard, and backyard. The house protected the only opening in the fort. The walls of the fort were three to four feet high. The kids who did not live on our street learned that the sidewalk in front of the Henry house was *NO MAN'S LAND. Walk here at your own risk.*

Very soon, we had no one with whom to do combat. Therefore, we had to make some enemies. Peanut and I harassed his brother Jimmy, as well as Dickey and Jamie, until they agreed to do battle with us. Never before had there been such a snowball fight. Those three boys were all a year or two older than Peanut and me. In our fort, however, they were no match for us. With our stockpile of snowy projectiles, we stood them down again and again.

The day school let out for Christmas was always a treat for the kids in town. The morning was devoted to an assembly in the huge vestibule-like hall. The kids lined up and sat on the wide, wooden stairway. A sixth-grader who could read well would recite "The Night before Christmas." One of the teachers would read the Christmas story from the Gospel of Luke. Each class sang a Christmas song. Then all the classes would join in, singing "Silent Night."

For the Christmas program of 1944, my class chose to sing "We Three Kings." Miss McNeal, who came to our school one day a week to teach singing, always chose the children to sing the solo parts. How proud and scared I was when she chose me to sing, "Myrrh is mine, its bitter perfume." I had no idea what myrrh was but I sang it anyway. I sang it beautifully in practice. When the day came for us to assemble and perform, my voice wavered, cracked, and then got real high and squeaky. I was so embarrassed, but I was hemmed in on all sides by kids, and I was too big to slide through the crack in the floor. Miss McNeal later patted my head and said that I had sung so well. Bless her sweet, gentle, lying heart.

After the Christmas program, the owner of the Avon Theater, Mr. Alexander, showed his appreciation for our patronage throughout the year by showing free cartoons and a very scary old movie of *Scrooge* to the children of all three elementary schools in town. We loved the cartoons. But we wished he had shown *The Three Stooges* instead of *Scrooge*. As we filed out after the show, a very thin Santa (who resembled Mr. Alexander) handed every child a small brown paper bag containing an apple, an orange, and some hard Christmas candy. We walked the four blocks back to the school building, where the teachers dismissed us for our Christmas vacation.

The year before, there was a huge fire in Adler's Department Store on the square uptown. It was such an inferno that fire trucks came from all the surrounding counties. They said you could see the fire from thirty miles away, in Indianapolis. It was almost like a fireworks display on the Fourth of July as the paint cans that were stored in the basement exploded and shot up through the fire and came down like mortar shells in the street. It was a sight to behold.

Well, anyway, debris from the fire was cleaned up and hauled away. A bare basement remained, which collected about six inches of water. Of course, the water froze the last part of November and remained frozen almost all winter. This basement became an ice-skating rink that winter. The older folks used part of it to skate round and round in slow circles. Those who wanted to practice figure skating used another section. About half of the basement became a hockey rink. Of course, we had no helmets. We used homemade sticks and a puck made out of a crushed tin can. Every kid in town became a hockey star.

That accidental skating rink kept our minds temporarily diverted from war that winter.

CHAPTER 7

BATTLING THE BULLIES

Leaving school one afternoon, I didn't have a care in the world. I made it through the day without a scolding from Miss Patterson, my fourth-grade teacher. She must have been in a good mood that day. I don't think she even smacked anyone with a ruler. I felt pretty smug about throwing a paper wad at Mary Wilson and not getting caught. Mary was the prettiest girl in the class. She had blond hair, blue eyes, and the cutest smile. Besides all that, her daddy owned a restaurant on the square uptown. I got her attention with the paper wad, and she didn't tell Miss Patterson on me. I guessed she must like me.

My cocky attitude turned to terror as I skipped out of the schoolyard and turned up the street. Waiting a block down the street for me was two of the meanest boys in town. They were twins. Bobby and Billy Arnold. (I guessed their mom didn't have much imagination when it came to giving them names.) These boys were not only mean, they were both cross-eyed, which made them look even meaner. Besides this, they always smelled bad and had runny noses. They were notorious bullies. When I was alone, I was fair game for them. This afternoon I was all by myself. My house was four blocks away. It might as well have been four miles. These boys were big for their age. They had been kept back a year in school, and they were in the sixth grade. I had heard they were dirty fighters. They liked to punch, kick, and bite.

Since I knew I couldn't lick them in a fight, I had to outthink them. Pretending I didn't see them, I walked with my head down. When I came to the edge of the schoolyard, I nonchalantly crossed the street. Coming to an alley, I turned and sprinted down it, quick as a cat. Looking over my shoulder, I observed two figures running as fast as they could after me. I had a good head start, and when I got out of sight, I turned the opposite way from my home. Taking a few long strides, I dove under a hedge bordering a backyard. In a few seconds, I heard heavy breathing and the sound of gravel crunching underfoot. I ventured a look through the leaves in time to see two figures turn up the alley toward my house. I lay there until my heart rate slowed to almost normal. Then I made my way cautiously through the backyards to my house.

This was a valuable lesson for me—a person should use their head instead of relying on brute force. No one got hurt that day, and no one got in trouble. I figured when you are big for your age and a grade behind in school, along with being cross-eyed, smelling bad, and a runny nose, you probably wanted to whip someone. I actually found myself feeling sorry for the Arnold boys. However, I didn't feel sorry for them long, because they would chase me several times after that. I always beat them to my front door where old Buck would be on guard. Reaching the refuge of the porch, I knew I was safe—because old Buck wouldn't let anyone mess with me.

The Orphan Bully

We had a strange group of kids in our school during the war years. We called them orphans. Some really were orphans, having no living mother or father. On the other hand, parents had abandoned some of these kids. These strange-acting kids lived in the Methodist Orphan's Home. They would come to school with tales of mistreatment. They swore what they said was true. However, as they told and retold these things, it became evident that they were lying through their teeth.

Hugh Munson was one such child. We called him Bullfrog. He talked with a deep, almost belching voice. He softened it some when he talked to the teachers. He was somewhat of a bully and wore wire-rimmed eyeglasses. They were so thick that they looked like the bottom end of a Coke bottle. He loved to pick on younger, smaller kids. He especially picked on kids who were from two-parent homes. I figured he was jealous. When he told us about how the people at the orphanage beat him with a big, thick, leather belt, I thought to myself, *good for them*.

Maturity has a way of changing one's opinion about things. Looking back over the years, I now understand that Bullfrog was a troubled young man. His daddy was away at war, and his mother had died in childbirth. Because strangers raised him, he did not like himself much. Perhaps things would have been different for him if only I had called him friend.

CHAPTER 8

THE WATCHDOG

He was never mean. He just protected his own people and property. That may best describe old Buck. He stood about knee high to my mother. He was white with a black saddle and black tail and paws. He had a brown mark above each eye that made him look like he was smiling. I have had many dogs since old Buck but none as good as he was. He could do a few tricks and would stay in any position I put him. He put up with me dressing him up in my old shirt and pants.

My folks never allowed any animal to stay in the house at night. The key word here is "allowed." I always figured what Momma didn't know would not hurt her. *It might hurt me, but not her.* So, late at night during the cold Indiana winters, I would sometimes sneak downstairs and let Buck in the house. He would creep up the stairs and sleep under my bed. On the nights Buck was under my bed, the monsters never showed up. It was reassuring to put my hand under the bed and feel his soft coat under my fingers.

We did not go off as a family together very often. We didn't have a car at that time, so if we did venture out as a family, we usually were not gone long. If my uncles came by and we were not home, they would pull tricks on us by setting kitchen chairs on the table or spreading newspaper all over the floor.

One day my Uncle Tom and his family came by to give us news about their oldest boy, Tommy, who was fighting in the Pacific. We had walked to town to buy groceries and weren't home when they stopped by. Tom and his family came on in and sat down, as they always did. Buck came in the house with them. He didn't bark or growl or anything. They sat for a little bit before deciding we might not be home for a while. They pulled their usual "chair on the table trick" before deciding to leave. Old Buck had a trick of his own. As they got up to leave, Buck placed himself in front of the door. Each time they approached the door to leave, Buck bared his teeth and growled in a very menacing manner.

When we arrived home, there sat my uncle and his family in our living room with Buck lying in front of the door. It looked like he was smiling, a very devious smile.

Old Buck taught them an important lesson: never try to trick a loyal family dog.

CHAPTER 9

WHISTLES AND BELLS

One April morning in 1945, as we were in the middle of Miss Patterson's math class, church bells began to ring and the Winkler factory whistle began to blow one continuous shriek. Shortly after that, the town fire alarm rang out. The sound went up and down in a way I had never heard before. Then a police car went slowly down the main street blowing its siren. Was it the end of the world? Was Japan making another attack on American soil? Suddenly, people were in the streets, all shouting at once. "Germany has surrendered. The war in Europe is over."

That evening Peanut and I were lying on the front porch on our stomachs watching some ants struggle to carry a crumb of bread down a crack in the walk. We were eavesdropping as Daddy discussed the headlines on the front page of the *Boonville Reporter* with Mr. Arnsman, our elderly neighbor.

"We still have to beat the Japs," Mr. Arnsman said in a calm, quiet voice.

Peanut and I looked at each other in a knowing way. I thought to myself, *Man, if we could beat the super race, we could surely whip those little yellow men with slanted eyes.* With eyes like that, Peanut and I were convinced they couldn't hit a bull in the butt with a canoe paddle. Whipping them Japs would be easy as eating cherry pie.

A few days before that, my Uncle Tom came by the house looking like someone had dropped a ton of bricks on him. They had just received a telegram from the War Department that Tommy was seriously wounded while fighting on some island in the Pacific. He was now in a hospital in Hawaii. That was all they knew about him. I still didn't know how the Japanese had wounded my cousin Tommy. They must have gotten lucky. He was a Marine Raider. I was sure he could have whipped a whole company of Japanese infantry. Tommy was just a farm kid of nineteen, but he stood six foot four and was tough as nails. I was certainly going to find out how they wounded him when he got back home.

Soon we began to think seriously about just how America would be able to defeat Japan. We saw in the newsreels how the Japanese fighter pilots flew their planes into our ships. They called themselves Kamikaze pilots. At the time I thought Kamikaze must be the Japanese word for "stupid." There was a rumor that these pilots knew how to take off and fly, but were never taught how to land. The rumor also was that they only had enough fuel to get to the target and that they were high on saké. However, the first casualty in time of war is truth. We really didn't have a clue as to the truth.

It was a very hot day in August 1945 when the bells and whistles again began to make their joyful sounds. This time the celebration went on for more than a few hours. I watched in awe as complete strangers kissed and hugged each other like long-lost relatives. Some even tried to kiss Peanut and me, but we were too fast for them. We made a hasty retreat to my old cherry tree. Yes, it was V-J Day. Japan had announced its unconditional surrender.

We soon learned this victory was the result of two new bombs that were dropped on Japan. When the newsreel showed the aftermath in the theater, we just couldn't believe two bombs did all that damage to two cities. Nor could we know that these bombs would change our own lives.

The era of the atom bomb was born. Peanut and I had a strange feeling of pride for our nation. America had overcome evil and saved not only our nation but also civilization. As the years went by, we knew America was right to end the war with two bombs named "Little Boy and Fat Man." We just hoped America had not created an uncontrollable monster.

GLOSSARY

Purple Heart A medal of distinction given to a soldier wounded in battle. It is also awarded to a family member posthumously.

Graveyard shift A working shift in a factory, usually between the hours of eleven o'clock p.m. and seven o'clock a.m.

Icebox An insulated wooden and metal box, which holds a block of ice and keeps food cool. Used before refrigerators.

Warm Morning Stove A cast iron coal stove used to heat houses before furnaces. "Warm Morning" was the make of stove.

Automatic Stoker	Used to automatically keep coal fed into a coal furnace. A large funnel-shaped hopper, which dropped coal onto an auger, which then fed coal into the furnace when needed.
Mortar Shells	A type of artillery missile used in war.
4-F	A term used for those who were physically unfit to serve in the military. Heart disease, flat feet, extremely poor eyes were some physical impairments that classified a citizen as 4-F.
Blackout	All lights in homes and business were turned off to avoid detection from the air. Candles could be used if one had heavy black drapes over windows.
Ration Stamps	The government issued these stamps to each family based on number of people in the family. It kept people from

hoarding scarce food items and reselling them at a higher price on the black market. For example, a family might be allotted stamps to purchase five pounds of sugar a month. You gave the grocer the stamp plus the purchase price of the five pounds of sugar. You could not "legally" purchase another five pounds until you were issued the next month's stamps.

Garand M-1	A World War II 30.06 caliber rifle
Grenade	Small anti-personnel explosives with shards of metal in them to inflict severe and fatal damage to the enemy.
German Luger	A 9 mm handgun made in Germany and carried by all World War II German officers.
Kraut	A German soldier.

ABOUT THE AUTHOR

Phil Emmert left a secure job at Dow Chemical Company in 1970 to enroll at Johnson Bible College in Tennessee. After graduation at age 37, he became a full-time minister. Phil continued to preach and was a social worker in the Department of Social Services in North Carolina. He later became a counselor in the county school system in North Carolina. While in this position, at the age of sixty-three, he began to write motivational thoughts for teachers and staff in the school system. He is the father of three sons and a daughter. He has eleven grandchildren.

    Phil's many experiences with young people as a father, grandfather, minister, children's social worker, and counselor have contributed greatly to his writings. As a counselor, he took a special interest in fourth- and fifth-graders. He observed that many of these children were not fond of history, focusing instead on current adventure books.

    Because of this, *When War Was Heck* was born. Phil began to write about his hometown of Lebanon, Indiana, during the Second World War, from the perspective of a ten-year-old boy. The characters are real, although the names may be changed and the events out of sequence. He adds the imaginations of a child to this story as well.

Phil Emmert combines easy reading with history, and seasons the story with homespun bits of humor and nostalgia in *When War Was Heck*. Phil hopes you've enjoyed these adventures including Peanut, Mary Anne, and Buck the border collie . . . and the events that influenced Phil's life as a young child.

www.ingramcontent.com/pod-product-compliance
Lightning Source LLC
Chambersburg PA
CBHW060505080526
44584CB00015B/1556